A MOTHER'S

Written and Illustrated by
MEGAN E. GILBERT

This book is dedicated to my children, who kindle the desire to "pray without ceasing." And it couldn't have been possible without the sustaining prayers of my loving mothers: Mommily, Mama Lisa, Mama Helen, Nona Maria, and Matushka ("Life Coach") Elizabeth.

In making this book, I drew together prayers from a variety of sources: the Holy Scriptures, The Breastplate of St. Patrick, the Akathist: Glory to God for All Things, and the Akathist to the Theotokos, Nurturer of Children.

A Mother's Prayer
Text and Illustrations copyright ©2020 Megan E. Gilbert

All rights reserved.
No part of this publication may be reproduced by any means, electronic, mechanical, photocopying, recording, scanning, or otherwise, without the prior written permission of the publisher.

PUBLISHED BY:
Ancient Faith Publishing · A division of Ancient Faith Ministries
PO Box 748 · Chesterton, IN 46304

store.ancientfaith.com

Printed in China.

ISBN: 978-1-944967-78-9

S WE STRIVE to pray without ceasing in days filled with thoughts of our children, may these pages help us to lift them up in prayer at ALL TIMES and in ALL PLACES.

LORD OUR GOD, who love my children so faithfully, bless each step they take this day and every day. Bless their coming and their going, their ups and their downs. Help us to know You as You walk beside us. Give me the wisdom to set a good example for my children, with true humility and without judgment, and to walk beside them.

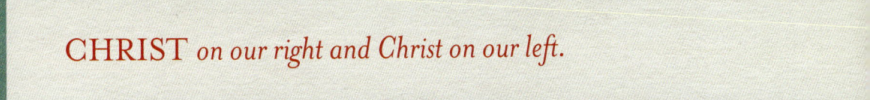

CHRIST *on our right and Christ on our left.*

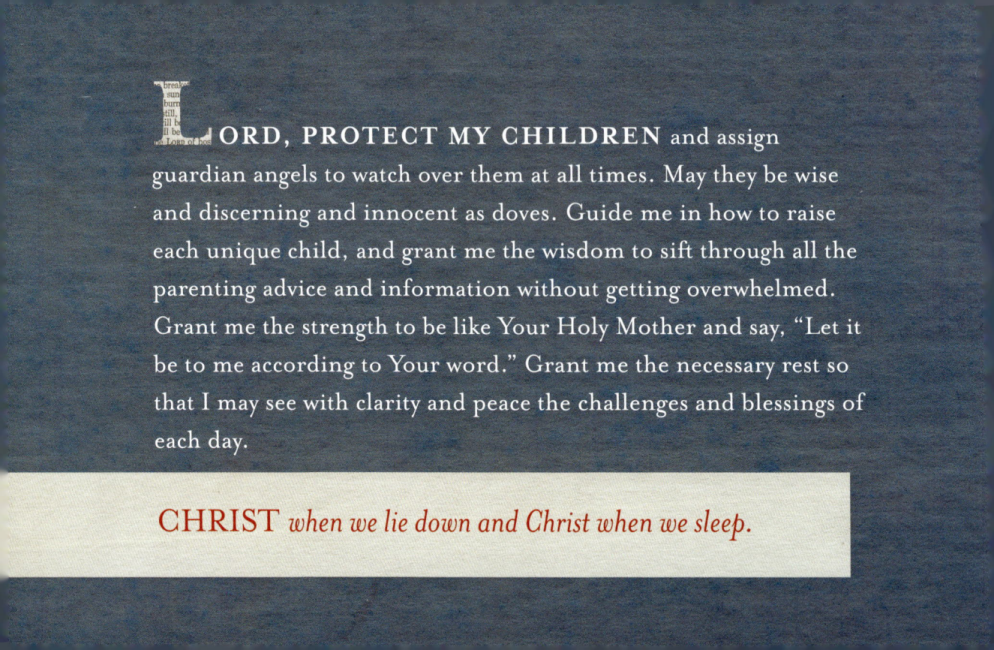

HOW GLORIOUS YOU ARE, O LORD, radiant with light, watching over us from the depths of infinite space as well as in the intimacy of our own hearts. Illumine our souls, fill our minds with Your truth, and open our mouths boldly to speak your praise.

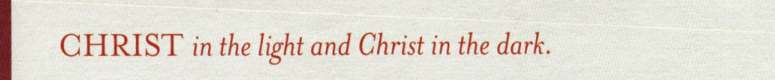

CHRIST *in the light and Christ in the dark.*

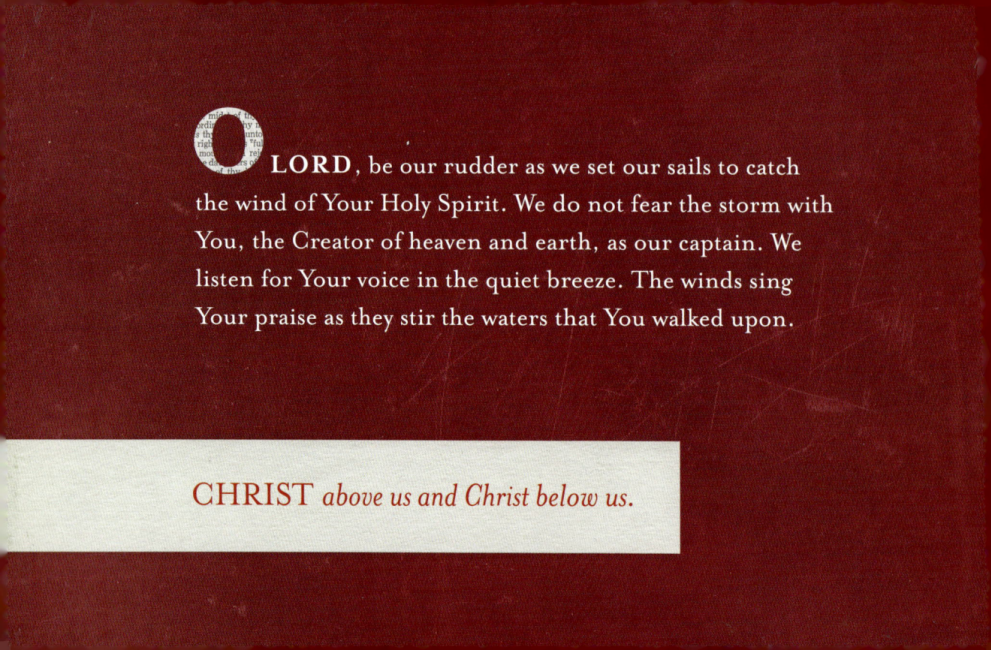

LORD, bless my children, who are made in Your image, to be living icons. Bind to them Your power to guide them, Your might to uphold them, Your wisdom to teach them, and Your eye to watch over them. Remind us to lay our cares at Your feet as we sing together, "Lord, have mercy."

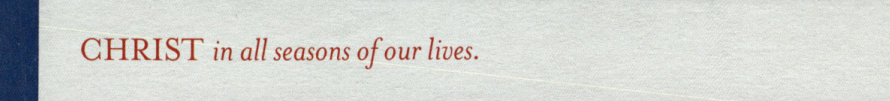

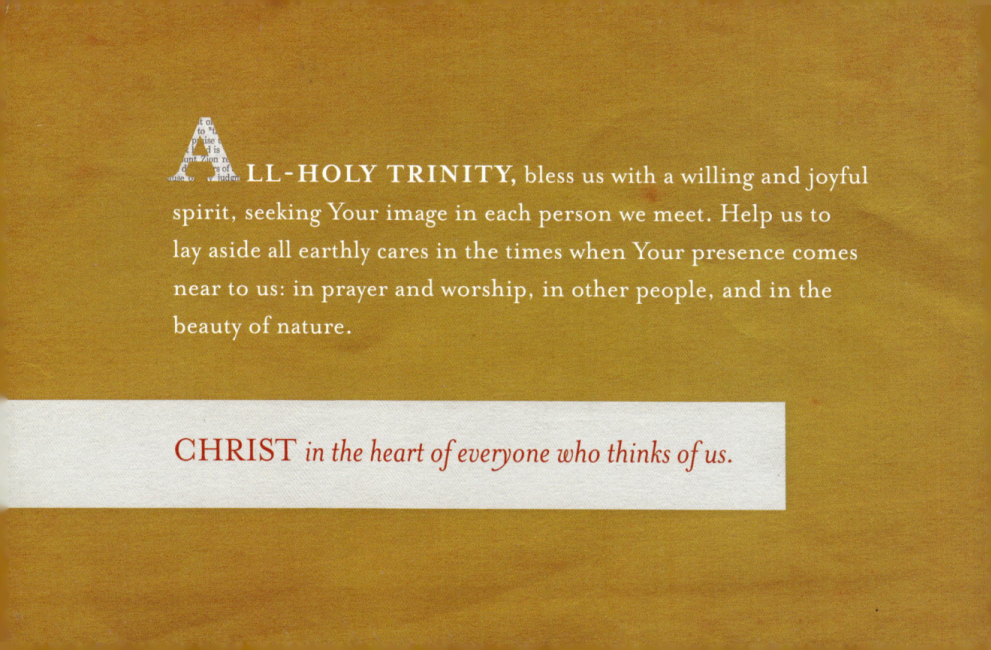

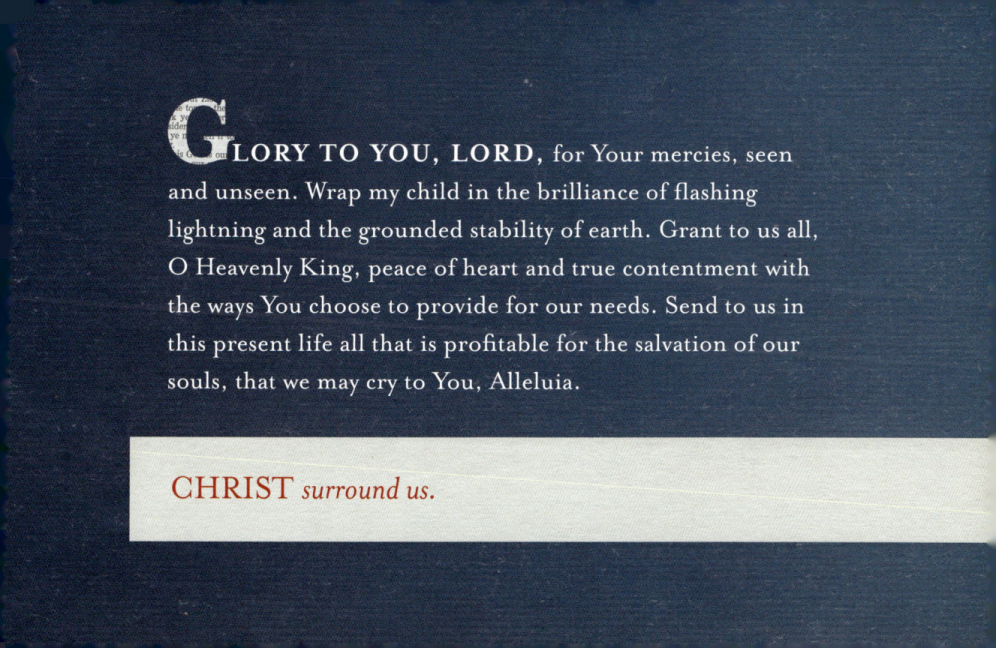

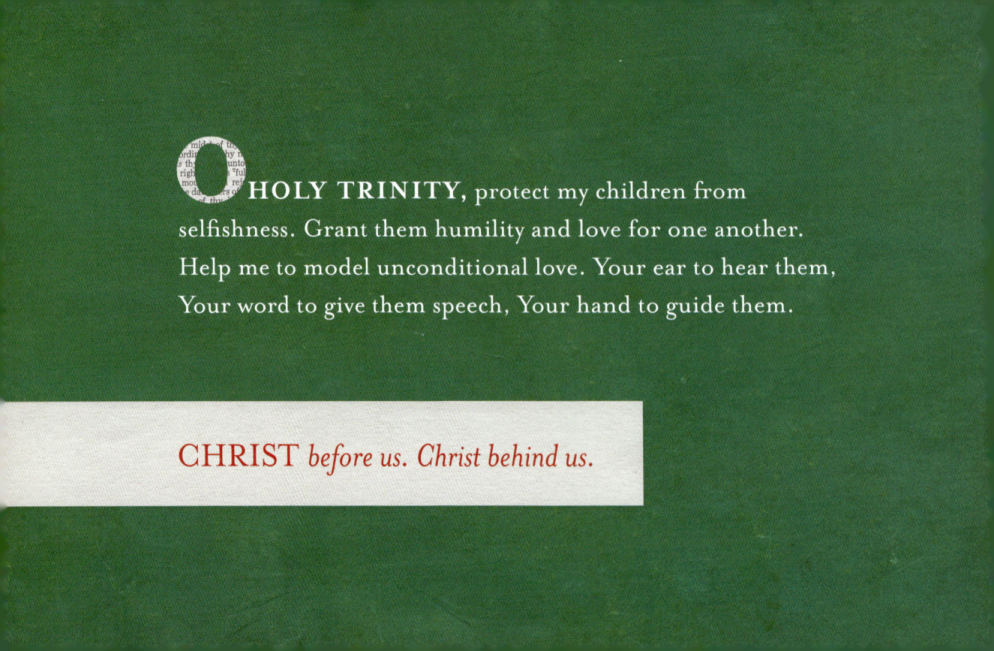

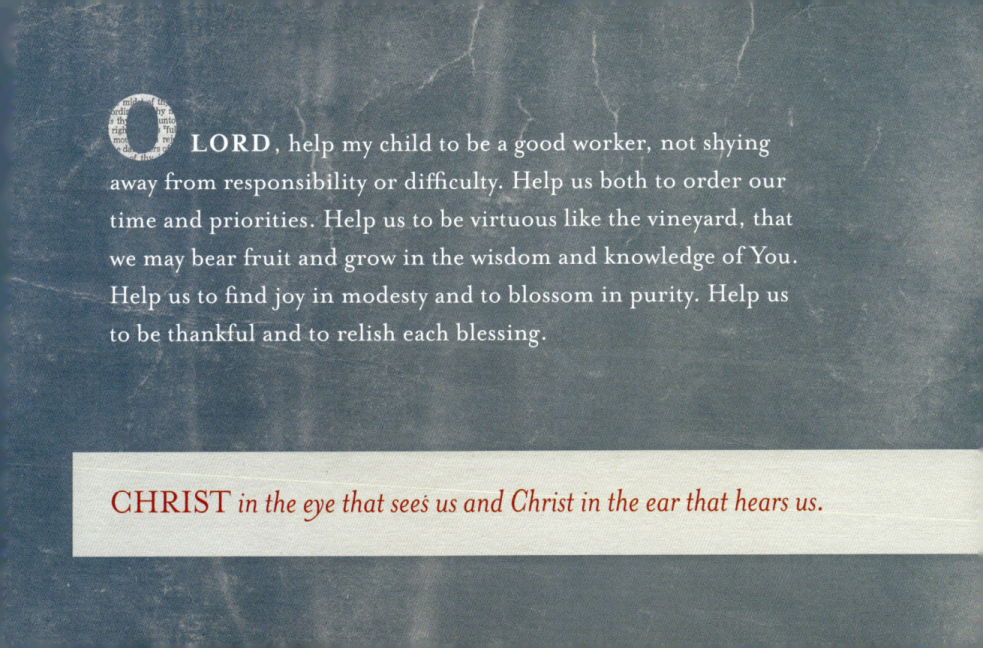

LORD JESUS CHRIST, I trust that all is sent by You and that everything happens for a reason. I pray for the safety of my children, but also trust that when some harm has occurred, all will come together for good for those who love You and put their trust and hope in You. Protect us against the tricks and traps of the enemy. Teach us to seek Your protection and take refuge in You. Help me to raise my children in the innocence of childhood, for to children belongs the Kingdom. Grant us to think, know, hear, say, and do only that which brings us closer to You, that we may sing to You, Alleluia!

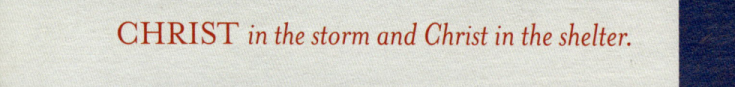

CHRIST *in the storm and* Christ *in the shelter.*

 LORD OUR GOD,
bless my child with peaceful and undisturbed sleep. Bring us peace as we gratefully pray to You. Make our hearts melt day and night with love for You, Your Holy Mother, Your precious saints, and our neighbors. To You we give praise, honor, and glory forever and ever.

CHRIST *within us. Amen.*